Washing Hands - Germs Children's Coloring Book

Educational Hygiene Coloring Activity For Kids Ages 3-5

Rachel Mintz

Copyright © 2019 Palm Tree Publishing - All rights reserved. No part of this publication may be reproduced, distributed, or transmitted in any form or by any means, including photocopying, recording, or other electronic or mechanical methods, without the prior written permission of the publisher, except in the case of brief quotations embodied in critical reviews and certain other noncommercial uses permitted by copyright law. Images used under license from Shutterstock.com

Germs are so small we can see them only through microscopes. In this coloring book you will see germs as they can be seen through a microscope.

Germs can make you sick!

After you visit the bathroom you have germs on your hands. The germs can enter the body through the nose, mouth, ears or eyes.

So the best way to keep them away, is to wash your hands with water and soap after being to the toilets and before you eat.
When you have germs on your hands you are spreading them to others.

Color these germs so you remember to wash them next time you go potty or before you eat.

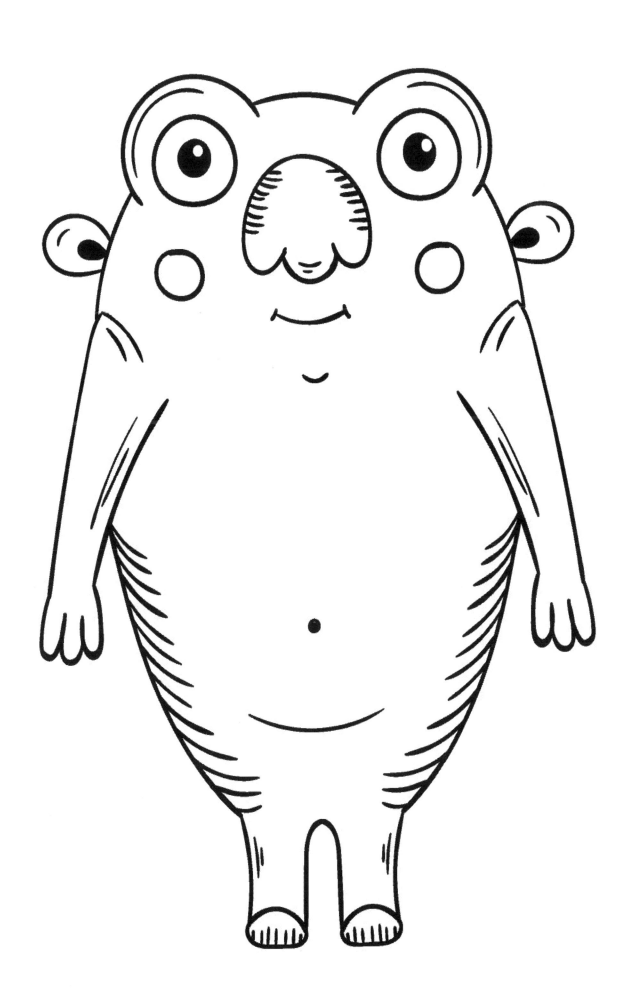

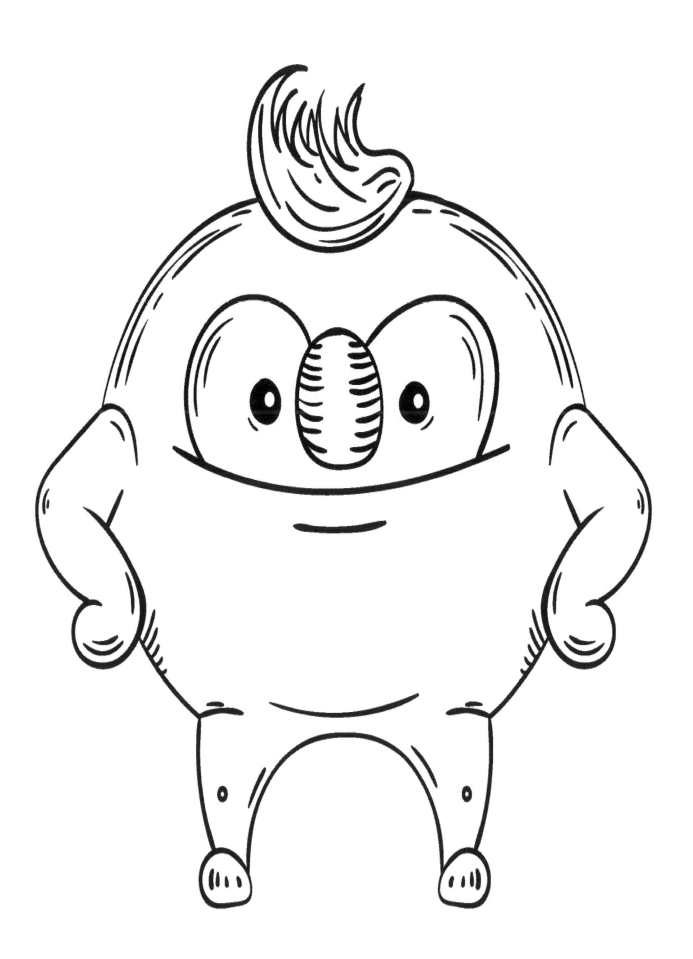

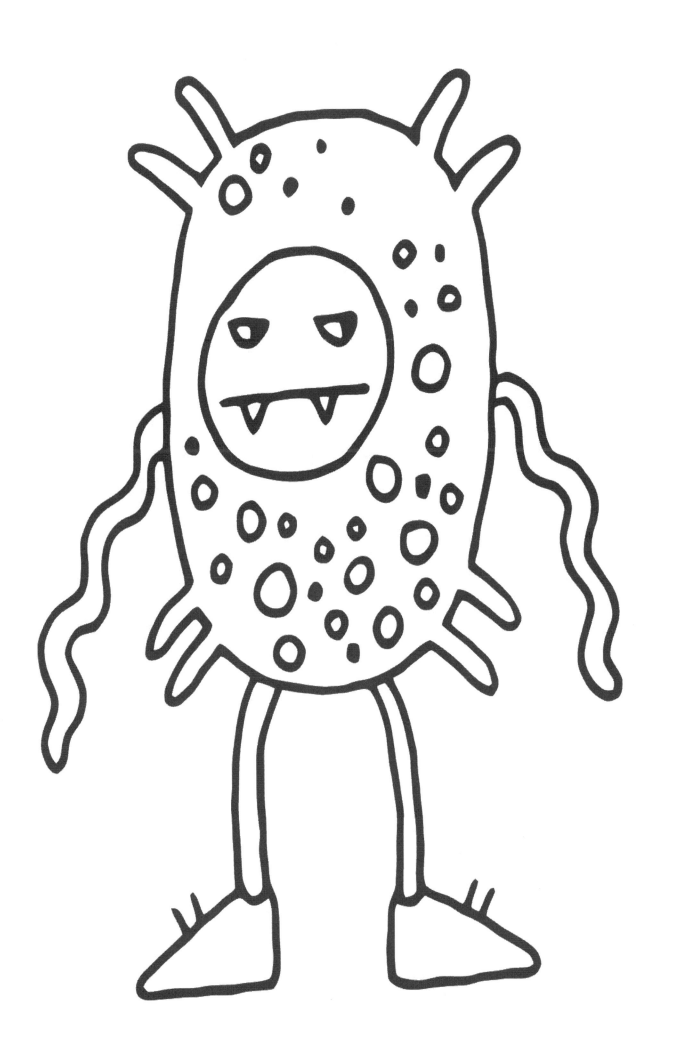

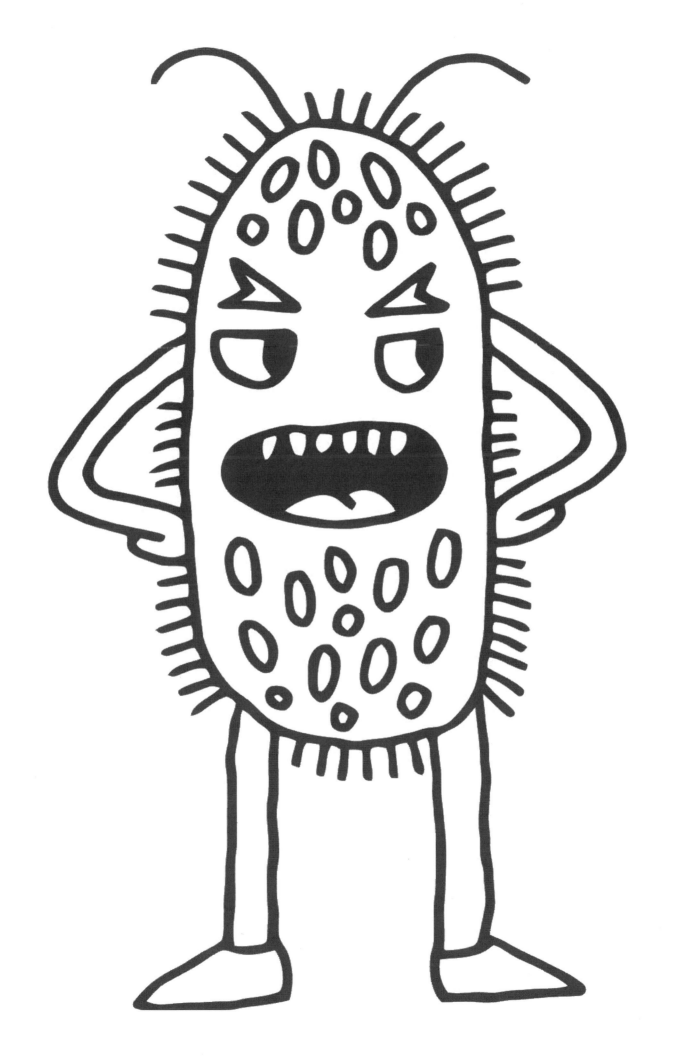

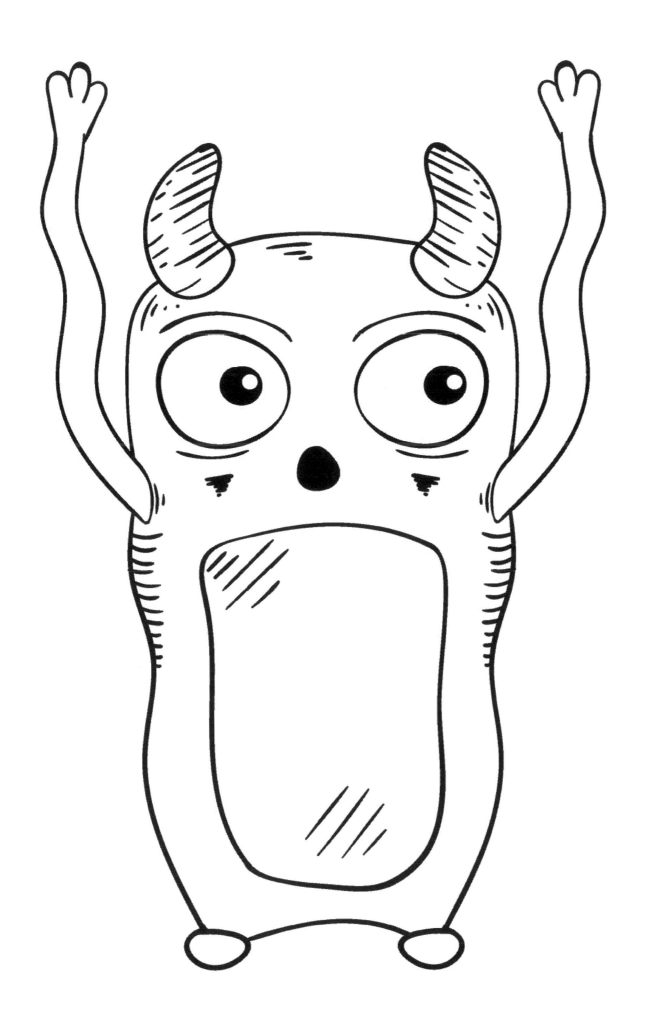

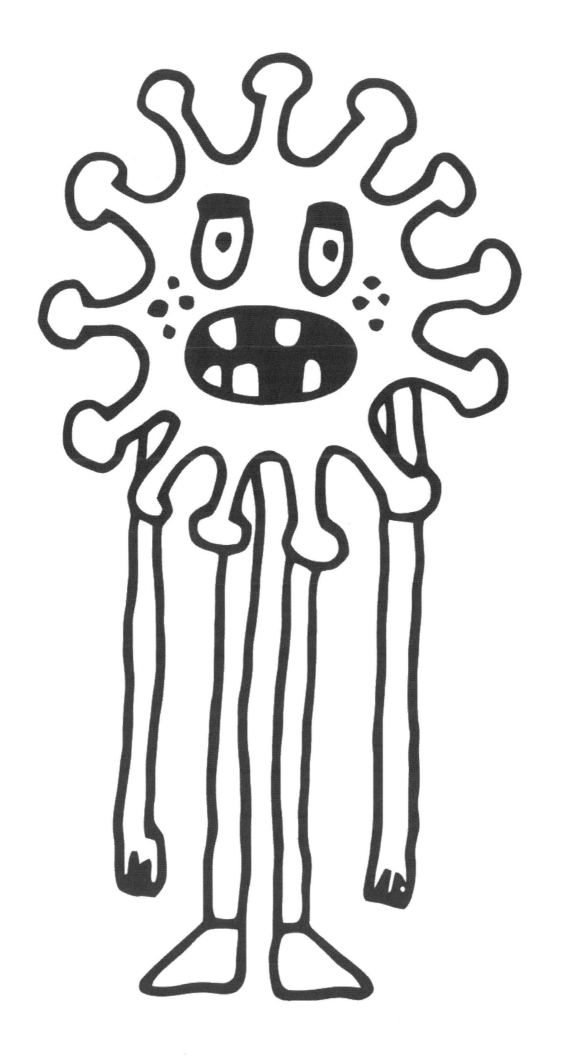

Thank you for coloring and coloring with us.

Please take a minute to review THIS book

More RACHEL MINTZ Coloring Books For You at Amazon:

RACHEL MINTZ Coloring Books

Drawing On Dots
Workbook for Preschoolers

Ages 3-5

Rachel Mintz

Hand-Eye Coordination
Trace The Dotted Lines

RACHEL MINTZ Coloring Books

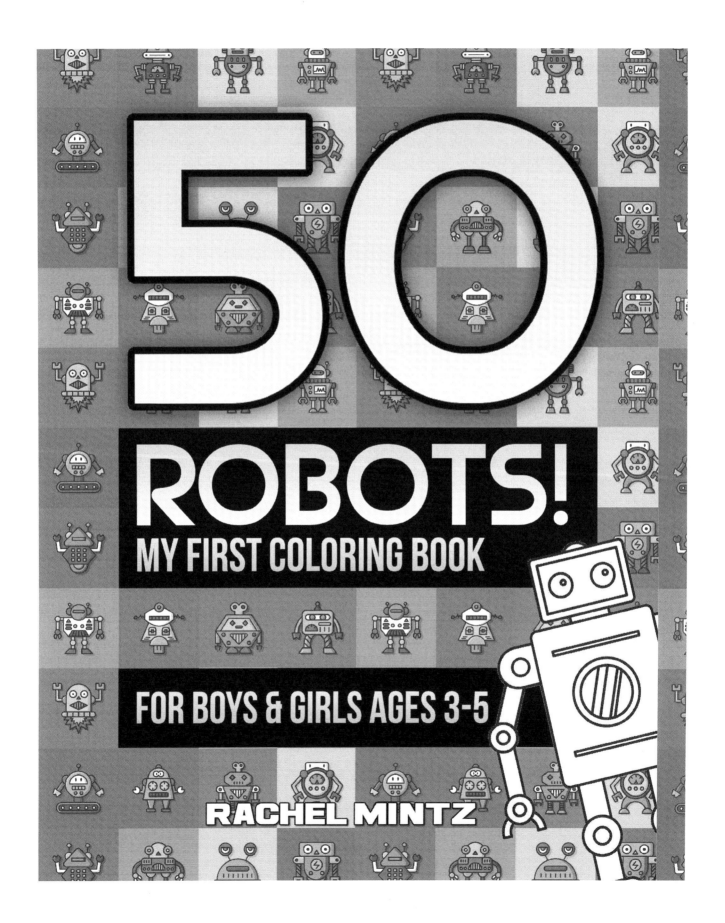

RACHEL MINTZ Coloring Books

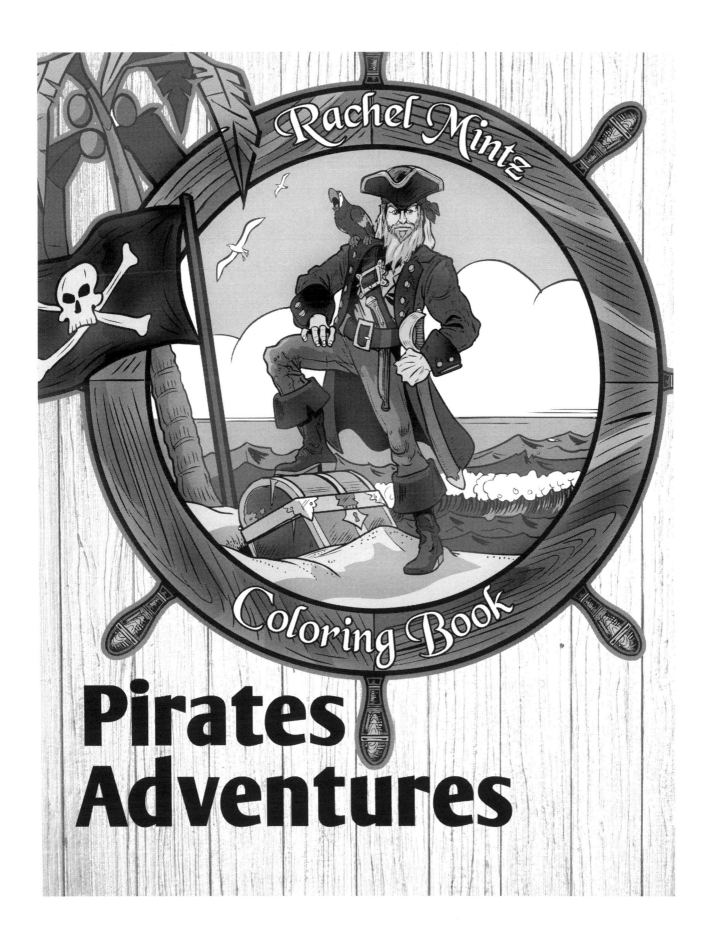

More Coloring Books For You

Mandalas | Wildlife | Marine Life| **Portraits** | Dogs | Cats | **Flowers** | Skulls | Gothic | Architecture | Romantic | Texts & Sayings | Ethnic | Steampunk | **Fashion** | Horses | Unicorns | Witches | Horror | Grayscale | Sports | Christmas | Holidays | Kids | Cars | **Motorbikes** | Trucks | Urban | Fairies | **Jewish Holidays**: Passover, Hanukkah, Purim | Safari | Pets |Multicultural | Educational for Kids | Back to School | **Preschool & Toddlers** | Army & Military | Knights & Castles | Dragons | Princesses | Butterflies | Birds | Reptiles | Bible | **Stained Glass** | Abstract | Machines | **Robots** | Space & Science | **Zombies** | Monsters | And many more topics..

Which topic would you like to color?

Search Amazon for 'Rachel Mintz + Your Topic' and find a book to color or as a gift.

Thank you for coloring with us

We will be very thankful if you could take the 60 seconds to review THIS book

Made in the USA
Middletown, DE
08 September 2022